Kingdom Woman

A Life Changed and a Purpose Revealed through Intimacy with Christ

BY

ADASUWA IYAMU

Watersprings
PUBLISHING

Kingdom Woman published by Watersprings Publishing,
a division of Watersprings Media House, LLC.
P.O. Box 1284
Olive Branch, MS 38654
www.waterspringsmedia.com
Contact publisher for bulk orders and permission requests.

Printed in the United States of America.

ISBN-13: 978-1-948877-78-7

Table of Contents

A book dedicated to all women,
for we are virtuous!

To God be the Glory!
Forever and ever,
Amen!

The Kingdom Woman Defined

A Kingdom Woman is one that allows herself to be led by God. This woman has vision and is secure in who God says she is. She understands her role in the kingdom and knows no limits, as she believes that she can do all things abundantly, exceedingly, and beyond her wildest dreams. She steps out in faith, puts her hands to work, and watches as God's beauty unfolds before her. A Kingdom Woman soars like an eagle, and when she does, how blessed the earth will be.

"BEFORE I FORMED YOU IN THE WOMB, I KNEW YOU; BEFORE YOU WERE BORN, I SANCTIFIED YOU."
JEREMIAH 1:5

Introduction

The most important decision I have ever made in my life was answering the voice of God when he called out to me. I answered "Yes!" Yes, Lord, I will follow you! Yes, you will be my God! That yes set the course for the rest of my life. There is one scripture in the bible that I hold close to my heart that is Jeremiah 1:5 it says: *"Before I formed you in the womb, I knew you; before you were born, I sanctified you."* That is one of my favorite scriptures! Take a moment and Think about that! To me, this scripture reveals the forethought God had about me before I was even conceived. Before I was placed in my mother's womb, I was in eternity, in the mind of God. How exciting is that?! Maybe that is why I was aware of the familiarity of his voice when he called out to me. Just a thought! On this walk of saying yes to God, I learned that we all have a choice. That choice is to step into God's abundance or to do what we will with our lives. Most importantly I learned that God's way never fails. Why is that? The Bible tells us that the footsteps of a righteous man are ordered by the Lord (Psalm 37:23). This tells me that God is intentionally guiding my life every step of the way when I choose to step into his abundance.

Do you see God as being intentional in and with your life? Did you know that before you were in your mother's womb God knew you? Maybe at some point in your life, you have felt the intention of God in your life but lost heart because of the waves and winds of life. Maybe you have never thought about how intentional God is concerning you. Maybe you know God's thoughts concerning you. Either way, I want to share my journey with you about the highs and lows of my life and share how I uncovered all the intentional actions of God. I invite you to see the innermost conversations that God and I had as He took me through a process of being called, sanctified, pruned, and arriving at the woman He intentionally predestined me to be. I want to share with you my journey with God revealing Himself to me one dimension after the other. Yes! God is not one-dimensional He is Alpha and Omega. I am that I am. We can never experience the fullness of that in one lifetime, but my desire is to get close!

I also desire for you to know and experience the depths, widths, and fullness of God for yourself! I desire you to know God's intentional thoughts concerning you and thrive in the person that He has predestined you to be. Throughout this book are checkpoints that are designed to inspire reflection about the intimacy of your relationship with God. I hope that you find them as helpful as they have been to me!

CHAPTER 1

My Journey to God

My dad came to America from Nigeria at 22 years old, prepackaged with all the customs and traditions of his homeland. My mom, a diamond in the rough, was born and raised in Newark, New Jersey. My parents were married for sixteen years, during which they built a comfortable life for their children. My dad was a hard worker, determined to provide security for his family. His hard work paid off, and he and my mom eventually purchased a home.

I considered my childhood home to be a mini-mansion. All the homes in my neighborhood were lovely, but my house stood out in novelty and stature. It had beautiful rectangular-shaped oriel windows, three floors, and a finished basement. Even more, it had a gorgeous, enclosed green and white porch that wrapped around the entire front of the house and a stand-alone two-car garage that matched the porch's color scheme. The house also had an additional living space, with its own entryway, that my parents rented out for extra income. All of this was ours! As a kid, the most exciting aspect of the house was the huge yard that surrounded it on every side. My three siblings and I played in that yard day in and day out until we were tired. I loved my house! The only downside was cleaning day when my brother, sisters, and I were tasked to make it shine from top to bottom.

We had full bellies, clothes on our backs, and a not-too-shabby roof over our heads. My parents had accomplished the "American Dream." Yet, I could not help but feel that something was missing. At seven years old, I carried a void that I could not at the time put into words. This void seemed to always linger within me. I did not know why, but for some reason, I never felt complete. For some reason I felt like some aspect of life was missing. While I didn't know what was missing, I felt like there was something more that I needed to know, or as if part of my attention was somewhere else, but how do you even begin to explain this at seven years old? When you have everything you could possibly want and need as a kid, where else can that void stem from? At times I pondered on the mystery of the void but trying to enjoy the beauty of childhood changed my focus.

As we settled into our new home, what seemed to be the perfect family relationship grew intense. From the outside looking in, we had it altogether-the big house, multiple cars, and not a need in sight; however, things were not what they seemed. There were intense arguments and lots of emotional instability. Fear had become an unwelcomed resident in our home due to my parent's dysfunctional relationship.

While I loved my father, I never knew what version of him I was going to get from day to day. Was it going to be the sweet, loving man, or the one that found fault in everything I did and reacted cruelly? The stress from his unpredictability made me wish I were somewhere else, away from the mini-mansion that I loved so much. One day I got the unrelenting side of him due to a situation that I did not deem punishable. This day I got in trouble for eating french fries. Yes. I said it french fries. I mean I knew my dad wasn't a fan of my siblings and I eating fatty foods, but I definitely believe I caught the wrath of his unpleasant day. After being yelled at for five minutes I went to my room and sat on the floor. I gazed out of the window, scanning the sky, searching for something, but I didn't know what or why. It often felt like something or someone was trying to get my attention, but I never got a definite vision. Although my dad's temper was forever wavering the one thing that remained constant though was that void. As months and months of arguing and disagreements between my parents endured, the void in me continued to grow deeper.

Towards the end of my parent's marriage, my mom began to attend church more frequently. We always considered ourselves Christians, but we were not avid churchgoers, only attending services once or twice a year. My mom began to take us with her to Sunday services, but I was more interested in hanging with the other kids that attended than hearing the sermon. Sundays became a day of fun for me; it was a time of relief from the chaos at home. Some Sundays, we would be in church all day, not returning home until late in the evening. I didn't mind though, because it meant that I didn't have to witness the bickering between my parents or get caught in the cross hairs of whatever inner demons my father was wrestling with that day. Our long hours at church eventually became another point of contention for my parents. My dad disliked that my siblings and I were getting home so late and having to go to school the next day.

As the months went on, the emotional uncertainty and

conflict within my family finally came to a head, and my parents divorced. I was 12 years old. I say the divorce was due to what I would call "a clash of cultures." My dad, while an excellent provider, was a harsh disciplinarian, which contested my mom's belief of "correcting in love." My dad's version of discipline and other issues strained his relationship with my mom. It also led to him retracting his love from his children when emotions became overwhelming. Despite the pain this caused, I was still a Daddy's girl, captivated by and filled with love for my father. So, when my parents divorced, it crushed me. I went from a financially secure, though emotionally dysfunctional, two-parent household to a life of uncertainty.

During the separation and divorce, my mom, siblings, and I moved a couple of towns over to live in a townhouse/office with my grandfather. Life was drastically different- finances were scarce since we were now living on one income. The court process coupled with an ugly divorce fueled my dad to go back into that mode of unpredictability, so that stream of income was far from reliable. Not only that I didn't have a space to call my own, everything just seemed to be turned upside down. To top it all off my grandfather made it a requirement that we attend church every Sunday. Church quickly went from being enjoyable to being a burden. Since I no longer needed an escape from home, I felt that I no longer needed church as a retreat. My siblings and I went from being excited and willing participants to begrudged attendees. After a while though, I started to be more attentive and began to consider what the pastor was saying. My interest in God grew. Hearing about this all-knowing, all-powerful God was fascinating, and I wanted to know more! So, I guess that requirement turned out not to be so bad after all.

Occasionally our church would host events, and since I was now fond of God I didn't mind going. One Friday evening, we attended a conference, where the pastor announced a special guest-a prophet. I had always heard that prophets had a God-given gift of knowing specific details of strangers' lives. In other words, a "true prophet" on first meeting a person, may be able to tell that person about current issues or conflicts they are dealing with, provide guidance about how to move forward, or reveal things that may occur in the future.

At the end of the service that night, the pastor invited people to the altar for prayer. I wanted prayer about knowing God on a deeper level, but I was also curious as to what the prophet would say about my life. Honestly, I wanted to see if this prophet was real or just someone trying to pull one over on everyone.

I walked up to the altar and waited anxiously as she went down the line, speaking over each person. As I waited, I prayed in my head, Lord, let her have a message for me, that is from You! When she finally got to me, we locked eyes. "God delights in you," she said. "When He thinks about you, He's just happy!" Then she added, "Don't be afraid of men's faces."

I responded, "OK" though I was truly confused by her last statement. What did she mean by being afraid of men's faces? On the ride home, I continued to ponder on what the prophet said. Although perplexed by her last statement, I was happy to hear that God delighted in me.

In the weeks prior to the church conference, I read the Bible and prayed by myself. Praying and reading God's word was all very new to me, so I often wondered if God heard my prayers and saw that I was making a real effort to know Him. That night at the service, I felt like God used the prophet to answer those lingering questions.

Later that night while flipping through channels, I came across a church service. As I watched, the pastor's face appeared to shift. When he turned his head left, it seemed like his face did not follow. There seemed to be a 6-second delay before his face would catch up to where his neck and head were positioned. He turned his head to the right, to the left, and again to the right. Each time, the face delay occurred. Assuming our TV was acting up, I changed channels, but there was no lag on the other stations. I switched back to the original station, and again, the man's face was shifting. My mind flashed to what the prophet had said about not being afraid of men's faces, and I became terribly afraid. I turned the TV off but still could not stop thinking about what I had witnessed. Had God been trying to warn me of this? Why did I just experience this? From then on, my desire for God grew even more intense, and I became especially intentional in my efforts to seek Him.

As I sought Him intentionally, I noticed that my mind would wander, and I found myself envisioning moments with God. In one of those moments, I imagined God was holding me as a mother would a newborn baby. I could see myself wrapped in His arms and engulfed in all His glory. Another time, as I laid down for bed, I imagined God looking upon me in delight. To be imagining these things at the time was a little strange since I wasn't fully sold out for God, meaning I hadn't yet made a complete commitment to living my life walking on the road of Christianity. Yet, I felt a closeness with Him, like I knew Him. I felt that same captivating love that I had for my father, for God. During one of my moments imagining His glory, a feeling of affirmation came over me. It felt like a declaration was being made and sealed at the same time over my life, but no one was there to witness it except me and God.

At that moment, I knew that I had a purpose in this world. I knew that there was something different, something greater stirring inside of me, and God was going to make it come to fruition. I didn't know what it was, but I knew it was something great. I had never imagined anything extraordinary for my life, so I had no idea how this purpose was going to be fulfilled. Even more, my current circumstances were not aligning with a life of greatness, yet I felt strongly that there was more for me. I held firmly to this belief, mainly because I needed it to be true so badly. My life had otherwise become the center of chaos and I needed to know there was light on the other side of it.

The move to my grandfather's house had thrust us into a new normal that, honestly, none of us were ready for. We pretended to have it altogether for the outside world, but we were struggling to keep things together. My mother was working a full-time job to support us. The financial burden and her trying to care for us alone was tough for her to manage. My grandfather helped where he could, but not enough to support four growing children. Being the older children, the brunt of the home responsibilities like laundry, cooking, and making sure our younger siblings' homework was done, fell on my sister and me. At the same time, my mom began a new relationship that we had to get acquainted with and adjust to, the new man in her life. This was not something that we were enthused about. We had no time to heal from the emotional strain and divorce of our parents before my mom remarried. We had just moved to a new home, in a new city, and now was this new man-our stepfather. It was all too much at one time, my siblings and I pushed back a lot. But can you blame us? All of this had happened over only six months! And as if this were not crazy enough, my grandfather's house went into foreclosure and we were evicted.

Over the course of a year and a half we moved sixteen times, from staying with family members, to getting our own place and losing it, and moving back in with family. I often felt that God showing up when He did, with the prophet's words and that feeling of affirmation, that He was fortifying me for all the obstacles I was encountering. I would think back to that night when I felt that sense of hope, that my life wasn't always going to be this way. Holding onto that vision, that future of goodness and prestige, helped me to maintain during those most trying times.

The years ahead would oscillate between hills and valleys. One minute things were going great and looking up, but shortly thereafter, there would be another pitfall, plunging my family and I deeper into debt and disappointment. With all of our transitions, I ended up attending several different schools. I attended two different middle schools and two different high schools, so it should be no surprise that I had a hard time building relationships. How could I? Each time, I thought I had gained a friend, it was time to move again. This continued with each school, but each time I had hope. I would start a new school and think, this year is going to be different! I'll make lots of friends! I'll join clubs and activities!

But it never worked out that way.

Most times, I ended up with enemies. I honestly couldn't tell you why I was the one picked on. I'm not sure if it was because I was on the quiet side or didn't have the latest fashions, but the conflicts with the other kids and me would get so bad that administrators would have to intervene. In mediation, they would ask the other student, why they didn't like me, and the remark was always something like, "I don't know; it's just something about her I don't like!" In one instance, a fellow student and I sat in the counselor's office after an argument between her and another classmate that I got pulled into over a false accusation of laughing. When asked what her problem is with me, she told the counselor she didn't like me, because my sneakers weren't white enough. Huh?! Bizarre right! I had always felt that I was a pretty cool person. Granted I wasn't as social as your typical teenager, but I was still down to earth nonetheless; so, I was baffled by all of the attacks and ostracism from my peers. These were also the times when that lingering and all too familiar void would resurface.

I believe my lack of adolescent relationships prompted me to commune more with God. I began to draw nearer, developing a personal relationship with Him. I continued to pray, read my Bible occasionally, and attend church when my parents made it mandatory. As this went on, God became a close Friend.

In 2009 my family and I finally settled into (Lakewood, New Jersey) and began to establish a sense of normalcy. I joined the basketball team in my junior year of high school. This was a big accomplishment for me because I had always wanted to experience what it felt like to have a "normal teenage life"-sports, friends, parties-all the things that seemed to be out of reach before. While the latter two activities never became routine for me, I actually enjoyed basketball. Most days, I would walk to the community court with gospel music blasting in my headphones. I would shoot around for a couple of hours, all the while singing and praising God. That basketball court became my place of peace. On the walk home, I would talk to God about my day or just whatever was on my mind. Talking to God became a part of my daily routine. Little did I know, the devil had his own plans for me.

Have you ever noticed that when you begin to form a relationship or gain intimacy with God, that something or someone comes in to distract you and knock you off course? For me, that distraction came in the form of the opposite sex. I think many of you can relate to that!

I was a junior in high school when I met Troy. He was not the type of guy that could stop a girl in her tracks. There was nothing notably eye-catching about him, no chiseled features or Adonis-like stature or captivating eyes. What he did have though, was a way with words. Troy could sell honey to bees! At least, that's how my 17-year-old brain interpreted it, and I fell hard for his slick talk. You know that smooth, nonsense that teenage boys learn from their older brothers or watching TV and rehearse! Deep down, I knew his words were empty, but to my own hollow self, it was music to my ears. After years of feeling isolated by my peers, it felt good to finally be noticed by someone. I yearned so badly to be wanted and needed. That yearning was about to take me on a ride I could have never imagined.

I was unaware of how vulnerable I was until I met Troy.

The insecurities and self-esteem issues that undoubtedly were festering in me for some time began to poke their heads above the surface. See, all these years I had been comparing myself to others. Does she have "better" hair than me? Is her booty bigger than mine? Why do I have to have brown eyes and hers are green? I wish he would look at me like he looks at her! Tell the truth! Some of you know exactly what I am talking about. It also didn't help that I was unable to mask my insecurities with material things, like we also have a tendency to do because my family had "just enough" to get by. I could not afford the latest clothes, shoes, and makeup to make myself "feel better". I lacked confidence, my self-worth was low, and I was longing to be accepted. Instead of running to God for affirmation, I looked to Troy for validation. Imagine finding validation in a 17-year old boy who doesn't even know himself, much less you! Despite this, I lived to please him and believed that his acceptance was something that I had to work for and earn.

See, although I was communing with God, I was unaware of my value in Christ. I wish I had rejected Troy and stayed the course with God; but, remember I did not have any friends and still ached to have that typical teenage life. Having a boyfriend would bring me closer to achieving that. In my mind, high school was supposed to be about being popular, creating unforgettable memories with friends, and fairytale relationships that ended with the girl marrying her high school sweetheart and living happily ever after. Couples like Troy and Gabriella in High School Musical, and Breanna and Arnaz in One on One had inaccurately shaped my view of high school. I finally had my shot at normality, and I was not going to let that go, even if it meant setting aside the only true, concrete relationship that I had ever built-my relationship with God. Why were God's acceptance and validation not enough for me?

The rest of my years in high school were an emotional roller coaster. Throughout our relationship, Troy lied, cheated, and diminished my feelings to me being "crazy", but I could not let him go! He was the first and only person that had shown any interest in me. What was I going to do without him?

My parents were very much aware of my relationship with Troy and all of its flaws. My stepdad would often tell me things that he said God revealed to him about the emotional damage my relationship was causing me. I knew he was right, but in rebellious teenage fashion, I ignored him and did what I wanted to do. I would get tired of Troy's deceitful ways from time to time and break up with him, only to be sucked back in by his sweet, cunning words. This cycle of sporadic happiness, but mostly heartache and depression, continued throughout my senior year of high school until I hit my lowest point. I was pregnant!

I still don't know why I lost my virginity to Troy, especially in high school. I had no intentions of being a sexually active teenager; I was saving myself until marriage. Yet, here I was, pregnant. How could I have let this happen? How will I tell my family? Maybe if I go to sleep and wake up in the morning all of this will disappear! The most prevalent emotion, though, was shame. I wished so much that I had heeded the warnings of my parents and the convictions I had received from God, but it was too late now. I had shamed God!

In my naiveté, I had no idea that the mention of "baby" would make a teenage boy run in the opposite direction-taking with him all the love, affection, and care he proclaimed he had for me. Yeah, I had heard and seen it happen to other girls but never thought it would happen to me. I was sick, still riding that roller coaster of depression and heartache, but this time, I was riding alone. I had no one to turn to! I had no friends outside of Troy, and my family would undoubtedly be ashamed of me. I had no other option but to turn back to the one Friend that I knew would always be there for me-God. Though, I was certain that He would also not be pleased with me.

For two months, I fretted over what to do about my pregnancy and came up with nothing. My child's father/ex-boyfriend wanted nothing to do with me, and I felt that my family would judge me. Time was running out. I had to do something. Young, scared, and confused, I decided to take matters into my own hands. I was never at peace with my decision. I knew God and what He stood for, so how could I deliberately go against Him? Still, I secretly scheduled my appointment at the clinic and waited worriedly for that day to come. I was full of shame, regret, and sadness. I remember spending those nights before my appointment just praying and crying out to God. All I could say was, "Lord, forgive me! Watch over my baby. I know she will be safe with you!"

The night before my appointment, as I laid in bed staring at the ceiling, I felt a pain in my stomach. They were mild pains, sort of darting across my stomach. I didn't think anything of it, but as the pain grew in intensity, I knew something was happening. The pain was so strong, I fell to the floor, moaning and curled in the fetal position. It felt like something was detaching from my stomach. Was I having a miscarriage?

My parents, who had no idea that I was even pregnant, had to call an ambulance for me. I was rushed to the hospital where the doctor later confirmed that my pregnancy had terminated. My shameful secret was out, and I had to face my parents. Surprisingly though, they did not meet me with judgment, but with love. We talked about the situation and decided to put it behind us. Since everything was out in the open, one of the conversations we had was what made me go the route of hiding the situation and what was learned from the experience. I often wonder if God lets things happen the way they did to save me from a lifetime of judging myself and living in a place of constant guilt. Maybe He knew that this circumstance would have kept me in a place where I would never be able to forgive myself had I gone through with the appointment.

That was a serious life lesson for me. I dusted myself off and started walking toward my future. I got a job, started community college, bought my first car, and my relationship with God was getting back on track. Things were going great, at least on the outside. Within me remained that void; the one that I had felt as an adolescent. Still new in my journey with Christ, I attempted to fill that void with superficial things: food, makeup, partying- which was an epic fail, because I stood out from the other "club" girls like a sore thumb! I felt so uncomfortable and out of place. One thing I know for sure is that the club is not my environment!

Once again, I had found myself in a sad, yet familiar place- no friends, no boyfriend, and feeling unfulfilled. My hopelessness was mainly exacerbated by the reality shows that I constantly watched. You know the Real (fake) Housewives of Wherever and the Dysfunctional Love and Hip Hops. You know the ones that suggest that if you don't have several guys in rotation; the newest, most expensive handbag; or weren't out getting "turnt" every night, that you must be lame. What a joke! But still, there I was absorbing all that nonsense and swallowing it whole like it was the living bread. Instead of continuing to fill the empty space in me with God, I fell back into my old habits, and right into a two-year, dead-end relationship.

I knew early on it wasn't going anywhere with Michael. In all the years we were together, he never introduced me to his family, never invited me to celebrate holidays or birthdays, and never really took me out on dates. He clearly lacked the qualities I wanted in a partner, but again, I had jumped at the first guy that showed me any attention. I would allow another two years of my life to be wasted in this relationship- cycling again through slivers of hope, heartbreak, and depression.

Like never before, I felt the Lord tugging on my heart. I could no longer put Him aside while I attempted to please someone who didn't truly care for me. I had to answer Him. So, I took a stand to serve and honor God first! I told Michael that we could continue to be together, but things would have to change. First and foremost, there would be no sex, of any kind, until marriage, and we both needed to spend more time in the word of God. He agreed to go along with these changes for the moment, but once he realized that I was unwavering in my decision, he wanted to break things off. This surprised me at the time because I had assumed that since he was 5 years older than me, that he would be ready to get serious and settle down. I know now, though, that it's not a matter of age but the condition of a person's heart that makes them ready for a commitment of any kind. I was 24 and could not believe the amount of time I had wasted on foolishness! So, in the summer of 2017 I told God, "Yes! I am serious! I'm here for You! Have Your way in my life!"

CHECKPOINT

After reading this chapter think back over the years to the moments that felt like God was pulling at your heart and trying to get your attention. Did you let Him in? What was your response in those moments? Do you remember what year you laid down your desires and followed Christ?

No matter what your answer was to this question know that God cares about you and causes all of your life circumstances to work together for your good because you love Him, and you are called to His plan and purpose. (Romans 8:28)

"AND YOU WILL SEEK ME AND
FIND ME, WHEN YOU SEARCH
FOR ME WITH ALL YOUR HEART."
JEREMIAH 29:13

CHAPTER 2

God the Wonderful Redeemer

When I told God to have His way in my life, it was not an immediate transformation. There were times when I fell back into cycles of sin with my ex and would end up feeling ashamed for continuously disappointing God. However, I kept pressing on, giving it all to God again and again. I started praying every day. I stopped listening to secular music and transitioned to nothing but gospel and music that was uplifting God. I hungered for Him more and more. Occasionally, I would look back in despair over how much time I had wasted by not following God. But I was certain, that through all the chaos and heartache I had endured, God was going to use me mightily. Somehow my life was going to be a blessing to others. Even though I could not see it, God was going to do something big!

Every Sunday I was in church. I was blessed to had found a place of worship led by a pastor that heard the voice of God and was able to communicate God's word to his congregation. It seemed like his sermons were written just for me. Whatever I was battling that week seemed to be exactly what the pastor spoke on. Can you say Divine?! I knew that God wasn't done with me, because He was actively feeding me. Just like a baby who needs her mother's milk, I needed God's word to nourish and sustain me as I grew in my relationship with Him.

I told God, "Lord, in the next couple of months transform me. I don't want to be the same person next year. Move mightily and reveal Yourself to me!" Sometimes, all we have to do is ask God for more of Him, and He will show up. He's just waiting for us to turn from the distractions of life and wholeheartedly seek Him. Scripture proves this to be true. *"And you will seek me and find Me, when you search for Me with all your heart"* (Jeremiah 29:13). Deuteronomy 4:29 reads, *"But from there you will seek the Lord your God, and you will find him if you seek him with all your heart and with all your soul."*

The next five months would be a testament to the Lord moving mightily in my life. I began to have dreams that I knew could only come from God. He poured out His wisdom, knowledge, revelation, and understanding on me. I went from needing and depending on the pastor's sermons to tapping into my own line of communication with God. Yes! I could actually hear what God was saying. It felt like a download of information, streaming into my brain. It wasn't an audible voice, but it was as if I could hear Him from inside of me. At times, God would speak to me during the week, and then on Sunday, the pastor would preach the very word I had heard! Honestly, the first time this happened, it creeped me out! I thought I was losing my mind, but when words kept being confirmed again and again, I knew it was God.

The Lord took me from a babe in Christ to a full adult in Him in five months. He is the Great Redeemer! He will redeem the years that we've lost if we allow Him to do so. People often feel as though they have fallen too far behind or "backslid" too far to get back to God, but once you say, "Yes," He will accelerate you spiritually to make up for the time you lost. He will ensure that you will finish your journey strong and right on time. I am a witness to that!

I had felt this way many times-that I was too late and had made too many mistakes for God's redemption. What I learned though, is that every day God's mercies are renewed. No matter how many times I fell, God was still God and His love, grace, and mercy would never run out. Once I made the decision to surrender my life to Him, He honored me by redeeming my lost time. The Lord is always there waiting, willing to welcome you back, to envelop you in a cocoon of love. I am a witness of the Lord doing this, and I believe He will do it for you and everyone who says "Yes" to His will.

CHECKPOINT

Let's talk about the wonderful Redeemer! What areas in your life have you experienced God as the redeemer? What about His mercies? The Bible tells us that the steadfast love of the Lord never fails, and His mercies never come to an end they are new every morning.

One thing, among many things that we all have in common, is time. How we spend that time is what differs. Some may think I've wasted too much time to be used by God, but I promise you it's not true. If you're reading this book or still alive on the earth today, you have time. One thing that helped me was a change of mindset. I read God's words and said to myself, "If He said it, He will surely do it".

I invite you to join in with the confession that changed my path:

Lord, I thank You for Your word. You said if I come to You, You will redeem the time the locust ate up. (Joel 2:25) Lord thank You for putting me on the path You set for my life. In Jesus' name Amen!

CHAPTER 3

Experiencing God

How many people have acknowledged God? Of those, how many have accepted Christ as their Lord and Savior? For those who have accepted Christ, how many have found their calling and purpose in God? Experiencing God will open your life to receive all of these things. I can truly say that it is an amazing feeling when you have your own personal encounter with the Lord!

When we experience God for ourselves, we become living testimonies to who he is. His grace and mercy become evident in every aspect of our lives. An experience with the Lord is a heart-to-heart connection that can look and feel different for everyone. For some, it is a moment of awe and wonder! While others have a more tranquil experience that just captures their heart. No matter the magnitude of the encounter, you will certainly know when you are experiencing God. Your heart is overwhelmed by his love and it is undeniable that your life has been changed forever.

I believe that experiencing the Lord for one's self is the most important moment in the walk with Christ. I say this because with every revelation, affirmation, or word that came to me after experiencing Him, I could be certain that it was

God's will for me and not my own desires. Experiencing God allows us to discern our own voice from His, thus ensuring that it is He who is ordering our steps. Moreover, if we never come to this moment of first experiencing God for ourselves, not only do we miss out on the fullness of who He is, but we are left to know Him through other people's interpretations and experiences, rather than having our own understanding.

In experiencing God and knowing him for ourselves, we learn how God communicates and relates to us personally. Yes! God handles all of his children in unique ways, just as a parent may handle their children differently. A mother may be more critical of one child and maybe a little more patient and forgiving with another. This is not to say that she loves one child more than the other, it's just that her children have different personalities and therefore require a different approach. God does the same thing in His communication with us. He may speak through signs, dreams, or imagery. Whatever the approach, God knows just how to tap into our uniqueness; after all, He is our Father and our Creator. No matter where you are in life, God knows how to reach you there.

Personally, I have experienced God mainly through what some might call intuition. He will simply place words in my spirit. What does that look like? For me, it feels like knowing an answer or having a sense of direction regarding situations that I have come to him about. I have also received instructions from God for how to move through various seasons in my life, but all of this came after I had experienced the Lord.

So, how do you get to this point of experiencing the Lord? I can't say that my experience with God happened overnight. I learned that there is a process that brings us to full restitution in Christ. There are three steps that take place when we invite the Lord into our hearts. The first step is justification, which happens immediately after we accept Christ as our Lord and Savior. Justification means that through Christ we are forgiven and made righteous in our living. Why do we need the process of justification, and what are we forgiven of exactly? Well, we are all born sinners, and there is nothing that we can do in our own efforts to make us righteous before God. Let us look at this in scripture. Isaiah 64:6 says, *"...but we are like an unclean thing, and all our righteousness are like filthy rags."* This means that even in our best attempts to live a righteous, honest, sinless, blameless, faultless, and worthy life, we will always fall short. Even our best efforts before God will still be as filthy rags. We needed someone to help us live a life that is pure and acceptable before God, and that someone was Jesus Christ. 1 John 2:1-2 says, *"And if anyone sins, we have an advocate with the Father, Jesus Christ the righteous. And he himself is the propitiation for our sins, and not for ours only but also for the world."* God has counted us righteous through faith in Jesus Christ, and through him, all of our sins-big, small, deliberate, and unintentional, are forgiven!

The second step is sanctification, which is the work of the Holy Spirit to conform us to the image of Christ. When we are in the process of sanctification-the action of making something holy (as noted by the Oxford dictionary) -we are set apart, and God begins a work in us through the Holy Spirit. This is seen in 2 Thessalonians 2:13. This scripture reads, *"But we should and are [morally] obligated [as debtors] always to give thanks to God for you, believers beloved by the Lord,* because

God has chosen you from the beginning for salvation through
the sanctifying work of the spirit [that sets you apart for God's
purpose] and by your faith in the truth of God's word that leads
you to spiritual maturity (Amplified version)." So, because God
has chosen us for salvation, sanctification sets us apart for the
work of the Holy Spirit to make us like Christ- ready to do the
will and purpose of God in our lives.

The last step in this process of restitution is the renewing
of the mind. This is a shedding of past thought processes
and stepping into the mind of Christ. Before we can do this,
we must understand that in Christ we are a new creation (2
Corinthians 5:17). A new creation simply means that we leave
our old way of thinking and living behind, and step into a life
with Christ. Ephesians 4:23 tells us to constantly be renewed
in the spirit of our mind. Verse 24 goes on to say that we should
put on the new man which was created according to God, in
true righteousness and holiness.

We can see how sanctification and renewing of the mind
are continuous occurrences that we as believers experience
daily. Our walk with Christ is a journey and not a one-time
event; however, from the moment of personal revelation of
Him, we begin to change from the inside out.

Over time, my desire for the Lord deepened, and I wanted
to know more about Him and His word. I started to yearn
for the things of God. That yearning lead to wanting to know
the mind of Christ and the wholeness of who He is. It was
my personal experience with God that led me to this place
of wanting to know more, and that is why it is important that
we all have that personal encounter with God. As believers
and followers, it is imperative that we learn all that we can

about God-His love, His ways, and His expectations of us as His children.

As we continue to grow in the Lord, we soon realize that we cannot live without Him. This is where we were created to be as His children. That is why scripture says, *"Man shall not live by bread alone, but by every word that proceeds from the mouth of God"* (Matthew 4:4). We will get to a place where we surrender everything to the Lord, because we want just Him! This an awesome place, because our eyes and our hearts are fully open to His glory and majesty.

CHECKPOINT

Have you fully invited Christ into your heart to be your Lord and Savior? When was the first time you experienced the Lord with an undoubtable heart-to-heart connection? If you are uncertain about your answers to these questions, don't worry. Accepting Christ as your Lord and Savior is as simple as saying:

"Jesus, I acknowledge You as Lord and Savior, I invite You into my heart to be my Lord and Savior, come in and transform my life for Your glory in Jesus' name."

CHAPTER 4

God Reveals Himself

As I mentioned, summer 2017 is when I started seeking God's face wholeheartedly and having Him speak to me. It seemed like every month He would show up in such a big way, and each time, I was struck with awe and amazement. I can remember one month of just feeling His presence in a real and tangible way. It felt like He was near, and that closeness helped me to walk in a peace and joy that I had never experienced before. There was a peace, knowing that no matter what financial hardship or relational conflict arose, everything was working together for my good, because I was (and still am) a child of God.

I will never forget the first time the Lord spoke to me; it was September 17, 2017. The previous week, I had decided to go on a Daniel Fast. On the Daniel Fast all meat, dairy, and processed foods are forbidden, only natural, plant-based foods are allowed. I also cut out social media and television. Normally, the Daniel Fast is performed for 21 days, but I decided to do it for only one week. For that week, my only source of entertainment was listening to my audio Bible and worship music. I was already doing this daily, but I just took it a step further by cutting out any other distractions. I wanted my focus solely on the Lord and His word.

From the time I believed in God, I had always wanted to hear His voice. I wanted to know what it sounded like and what it felt like when you heard the voice of the Creator of the Universe. The Bible is filled with people that the Lord spoke to. For example, Abraham, Moses, Elijah, and Paul all heard the voice of God. I would often hear pastors say, *"The Lord told me..."* or *"The Lord spoke to me and said..."* Well, if God can speak to all these people, can He not speak directly to me? So, I set a goal that week of fasting. I was going to separate myself from the world and hear the voice of the Lord.

I started my fast on a Monday. The first three days consisted only of worship, work, school, and Bible study. I felt good about how the fast was going; I was hanging in there, eating only what I should, and studying the word consistently. On Thursday a thought popped into my mind. *I wonder what will happen if I go the next two days without eating anything-just water and the word?* So, I committed to doing just that. It was not easy. At the time, I was working at White Castle. I worked eight-hour shifts surrounded by tiny, juicy burgers, hot french fries, and sweet, creamy milkshakes! Those days were hard, but my spirit desired God more than my body desired to indulge its fatty, sugary cravings. I had to fight against my flesh to let my Spirit prevail. In hindsight, this was a lesson in and of itself. On this journey, we will have to deny our flesh much greater things than food.

Friday night, I felt impressed to go shopping for a girl that attended my church. This young lady was someone the Lord had used to minister to me. She is part of the reason why my fire for God became a burning flame again. Not only did she minister to me with her words, but through how she lived her life and her daily walk with God. One day she had walked into church and seemed to have a glow surrounding her as if there was a small piece of the sun behind her. She convicted me with her presence alone. Not only did I feel conviction, but I saw hope. Hope that I could get back to the place that I had fallen from. In those months before and throughout my fast, she held my hand and helped me grow spiritually. She literally bore my weakness and helped me grow in God. Her bearing my weakness means that she saw where I was on my spiritual journey and offered her assistance in helping me learn how to study the Bible and seek God. She held my hand through it all until I was able to stand on my own. Because of this, I wanted to find a way to thank her without looking cheesy. I had planned to get her a gift a few weeks prior but feared it would make me look awkward.

That Friday night though, I felt compelled to get her something to show how much I appreciated her friendship and guidance. I went to Staples and purchased a gift card since she had mentioned that it was one of her favorite places. I bought her favorite candies and a thank you card. The card was beautiful and said everything that I wanted it to say, and it was the last one in stock. Thank God for His divine timing!

The following night was the last night of the fast, and I started to feel discouraged because I felt like I had not yet heard the Lord's voice. As I sat there putting the young lady's goodie bag together I read the card again, and although it was perfect, I wanted to write her a letter that really embodied my heart. As I sat there at midnight writing this letter, it felt like a stream of words began to flow from the sky and into my mind.

I will never forget that feeling! I captured each of those words and let my pen scroll across the page. This letter had perfectly illustrated my feelings. However, I was still reluctant to give it to her. People of my generation do not write letters, much less a letter to a friend to show gratitude. I was worried that she would think of me as a weirdo, but I wasn't going to let fear stop me from what God led me to do.

Sunday came, and I walked into church with the gift bag in hand, waiting to give it to my friend after service. The pastor's sermon that morning was titled: Bearing the Weak. He talked about how our walk with God is all about being mature in Christ, grabbing the hand of someone who backslid or is new to the body of Christ, and helping them grow in God. He went on to say, that eventually, we should let their hand go, and push them forward so that they can walk on their own; and, that we should repeat the process with as many people as we encounter who needed and wanted to know God. I sat in shock! He was saying exactly what was "downloaded" to me the night before. I could not believe that the pastor was preaching almost exactly what I had written to the young woman. *My God! I had actually heard what God was saying!*

After service, I found my friend, gave her the gift bag, and told her to open it when she got home. Of course, she didn't wait and texted me ten minutes later to tell me how much the letter had blessed her. I began to cry. My heart was so overwhelmed with joy. First, to know that God hears me and honors my prayers. Second, to know that I had been a blessing to someone who I felt was leading me.

No matter how we think we may be perceived, when God is leading us to do something, we just have to do it! I often wonder what the outcome would have been had I let fear stop me from giving her the gift that day. Maybe I would have gotten the courage to give it to her another time, but it probably wouldn't have had the same impact as that divine moment. To be able to edify and pour back into someone that helped me grow felt awesome! My Daniel fast held a double blessing for me- I had heard God's voice, and I was able to uplift someone that I considered a mentor. I was so thankful, grateful, and honored for my personal encounter with God, that I began to seek His face more and more. He continued to show Himself so real to me month after month.

Although that was awesome, God's voice didn't just magically come to me after that one week of fasting, however. I had spent much time in His presence before my fast. Daily, I forced myself to wake up at a time that was uncomfortable for me to commune with God. I would've much rather been sleeping at 4 a.m., but to chase God, I rose early and spent an hour alone in worship. Remember, God is ready to be glorified through you! How hard are you willing to seek Him? What sacrifices are you willing to make to experience His glory? As you begin to press into His presence and relentlessly seek His kingdom, I know He will reveal Himself to you. He did it for me!

CHECKPOINT

Wow! God is so intentional in wanting to reveal Himself to us. Have you experienced a moment when God revealed Himself to you? Have you ever desired to hear the voice of the Lord? The desire to hear God's voice became a real desire to me when I started seeking the fullness of who He is. I desire to know God much deeper now. Remember the Lord said if you seek Him you shall find Him. Be encouraged and know that God will honor your desires to know Him.

CHAPTER 5

Season of Wilderness

Twenty seventeen was a great year for me. The more time I spent in God's presence and continued to delight myself in Him the more He revealed Himself and who I am in Him. He showed me detailed glimpses of my purpose-the reason He created me and my heart was overwhelmed with joy. This special time with God was amazing, though I still faced life stressors.

There were unnecessary issues with coworkers, family feuds, and the burden of juggling college tuition and other living expenses, but knowing that I had God on my side made it so much easier to deal with these challenges. I felt so empowered. I learned to walk in God's forgiveness, pray for my enemies, and even support my enemies, which really took the strength of Christ.

In January of 2018, my spiritual progression was at an all-time high. At this time, I reconnected with a high school associate, and they invited me to their church where two people prophesied to me. The first person was brief in his explanation, but the second went in-depth about my past, present, and what God was saying about my future. Everything this person said confirmed the desires of my heart, and what I believed God was saying to me. At that moment I thought my life would be accelerated to a new level. I thought I was on the fast track to a life free of trials and tribulations because of my new ability to prevail in the face of opposition. I was unaware of the season of wilderness I was entering. I had failed to remember that we will always have tribulation, but Jesus Christ has given us the strength to overcome (John 16:33).

February 2018 proved to be a repeat of my teenage years-times of uncertainty dotted with fragments of hope. I would often see an inkling of light at the end of the tunnel in some of the dark times, but then as I would draw nearer, things would fall apart. I felt trapped in that cycle for years, whether finances or family goals-any step forward was always curtailed.

That month my mom announced that she wanted a divorce, shut off notices and eviction pending, and again our family was thrust into the unknown. As a last and only resort, my mom, sister, and I moved in with my older sister and again things in the home were tumultuous. It was my last semester of college, I was working full time, and still struggling financially to make ends meet for my family and myself. If that was not enough, my mom became ill. She developed what is called low-grade sarcoma which caused a tumor to grow in her stomach wrapping around her organs. At the time she couldn't work because this tumor was sucking all of her energy and nutrition and in the physical, she looked as if she was nine months pregnant. Since my work schedule was more flexible than my older sister, I was the one taking my mom back and forth to doctors' appointments and still trying to make it through my last classes. After a few months, it came to the point where my mom had to have a thirteen-hour surgery to remove this sarcoma. All went well with the surgery but there was a two-month road to recovery. It all became too much; I could no longer endure the stress and the burden of supporting my family. I craved peace and needed it even more! Seven months after moving into my sister's house, I left to go live with a friend. Over the next eight months, I went from being confident in God-regularly seeing and hearing Him-to silence. *What happened to the promises that were declared over me?*

Despite having moved in with my friend, I felt confused, alone, and depressed. There were many days where I had just enough energy to go to work and would sleep the rest of the day. I began over-indulging in food to numb the pain and disappointment of what my life had become, or should I say, had not become. Overeating and sleeping were my new normal. My life was in such disarray. *Why would God tell me all these wonderful things about my future, for nothing to pan out?* Instead of being accelerated into those promises, my life was stagnant. I was so resentful towards God that I couldn't even pray. Things continued in this way for months, until one day, I mustered the strength to speak to Him. "God, what is happening here? Show me where I went wrong!"

I did not hear him speak immediately, but as the days and weeks went on, He began to expose the errors in my heart. He was uncovering one fault after another; it was as if He was saying to me, "This is the season I'm going to get all that 'stuff' out of you." He showed me characteristics that I never knew I had-pride, contention, and even lack of faith. This entire time, I had been withholding certain areas of my life from God.

I consider myself a strong person. I can endure through

much of what life throws at me, but this process of "pruning" that God was doing in my life, I had no control over. He was reaching into the deepest parts of my soul and extracting those things that I, and so many of us, had become accustomed to carrying, even when they are harmful to our well-being. Some refer to it as "baggage"-the stuff we hide from the outside world and try to convince ourselves that it's normal or acceptable. However, when God grabs a hold of those hidden pieces, it changes how you view them. You can no longer carry them comfortably, and God was stripping my pieces away, one thing after the other. It felt like I was unraveling from the inside out.

I was so angry with God that some days I would debate about attending church. *Who would have thought that the girl who eagerly and faithfully attended church three times a week would be feeling like this?* I remember feeling so defeated one Sunday morning that I had resolved to stay in bed all day. As I tried to force myself back to sleep, I heard a gentle but loud voice repeat, "Adasuwa, the Lord is with you! Adasuwa, the Lord is with you!" I could literally feel the heat of breath next to my ear as the words were spoken. I rallied the strength to get out of bed that day, but I was still not fully convinced that the Lord was near. *If He was near, why was I still feeling like this? Was it really necessary to expose the errors of my heart? Why, after being so present, suddenly go silent? Was it because I was finally alone?* Because for once in my life, it really was just me and God-no more family conflicts, no more expectations of supporting other people, no more having to operate in superpower mode. I could finally take the cape off, focus on myself, and be face to face with God.

As I labored through Bible study one day, I came across

Matthew 3:13-17. These verses illustrate Jesus's baptism. It reads that after He came up from the water, the heavens opened, and the Spirit of God descended upon Him like a dove and alighted upon Him. Afterward God says, "This is my beloved Son, in who I am well pleased" (Matthew 3:17). The first line of the next chapter goes on to say that, *"Jesus was led into the wilderness by the Holy Spirit to be tempted by the devil"* (Matthew 4:1). I thought to myself: *After such a significant moment where Jesus is affirmed by the Father, why does He have to go into the wilderness?* If I was writing the story, I would have had Jesus casting out demons, healing the sick, and doing miracles from that very moment!

I can see now how I had been applying that same narrative to my own life. I thought that after the Father had made the verbal announcement over my life, that everything would be smooth sailing from then on. Immediately though, God led me into the wilderness. Isn't that just like us, to create our own stories for our lives? That is one of our greatest faults and sources of disappointment. It is us painting pictures in our minds of what our lives should be instead of letting the Father have full control and lead us in our journeys.

I often wonder what Jesus's thoughts were in the wilderness. Did He ever look at the Father and wonder why He was there? In Matthew 4, the Bible tells us that Jesus fasted for forty days and nights, and afterward He was tempted by Satan. When I went into my own wilderness, there were days I felt so strengthened and affirmed in who I was in the Father, but there were also days where I felt like life was caving in on me. One thing that I learned in that season and am still learning, is that God is the author of our lives. I may have an established timeline for myself, but ultimately, God's timing is perfect.

I continued to have highs and lows. I also began writing poetry. I wish I could tell you this long elaborate story of where my desire came from to write poetry, but I can't. All I can say is one day I heard a poem in my spirit, and I began to write what I heard. All of my poems literally fell into my lap. I wrote with little to no effort of my own. I now have upwards of twenty poems about the Father in my collection and am still writing when my Spirit receives a word. Here is a poem I wrote during the summer of 2019, that completely expresses what I was going through in that season.

The Wilderness

Lord, I looked for You in the sky
My soul wept because I couldn't find You
My mind intervened and said see He left You
But my Spirit reminded me the Father said
He will never forsake me
What is this season Lord where I can't hear You?
I'm lost in need of Your guidance just to breathe
Take my hands, my God
Lead me in the way of Your perfect plan
I'm desperate to hear from You again
In this season I cling to You
Holding on to Your words and promises
Lord comfort my heart as I walk through this
Wilderness

This season in the wilderness prompted the desire to delve even deeper into who God really is. I wanted to know the fullness of His love, His nature, and His identity-my Father the Creator of the Universe. Of course, on an intellectual level, I knew these things about God. We learn about them during Sunday services or when we read the Bible, but I wanted to know Him intimately. I felt like I was only scratching the surface of who He was.

There's a difference between knowing who God is and really being captivated by the fullness of who He is. In this time, it was as if God was pulling back His own layers, so that I may know Him fully and never again waver or question who He is. Above all, I clung to the fact that He is an inseparable Father. I clung to all that He is! God being an inseparable Father penetrates my Spirit so deeply because it opposes my relationship with my earthly father.

My dad, although a great provider, would at times withhold love. One day, I would be his baby, his precious child; and the next day, I would be a disgrace, a failure, or just not good enough. I didn't realize how his words impacted me. I didn't realize that this made me feel like I only deserved love when my actions were pleasing to him. I had to strive to earn his love. The worst part was that I had placed these same expectations on my relationship with God; I was projecting what I experienced with my earthly father onto God.

I felt like when God was happy with me, I was His beloved child. If I did something against Him, I felt like He threw me away and didn't want anything to do with me. I thought God would deny me of His love until I did something to make Him happy again. This would cause me to shy away from

God's presence when I had done something that I thought was displeasing to Him. I was living as though God's love was conditional. During my wilderness season, God completely shattered that mindset. I learned that God is not a fair-weather Father. He is love! When we sin, we are supposed to run to Him-not in the opposite direction. He is a good, loving, and devoted Father!

In maturing, I learned I could not blame my earthly father for his actions; someone cannot give what they never received. If you know anything about Nigerian culture, you know that African parents can be tough. Not all, but some parents are more prone to display disappointment rather than praise, even when their child is doing the right things. One day in conversation with my dad, he shared how his mother disciplined him intensely to make him a better, more successful person. This conversation took place years after the divorce.

At that moment I started to recognize the pattern between his upbringing and ours as his children. Consequently, he only knew to raise me and my siblings in the same way. After hearing this, everything started to make sense. He wasn't a bad father, but his way of ridiculing and chastising had been ingrained in him since he was a child.

The peace and love that God had allowed me to experience opened my heart to understand life from my dad's perspective. Although his way of communication wasn't the most sincere or effective, he loved and wanted the best for his children. My father, like all humans, was not perfect. I found that perfection in my Heavenly Father; He is consistent, committed, and loves me without restraint! To know and have experienced this makes my heart leap with joy! God is so wide and vast that I don't believe anyone can experience the fullness of depth of the love that comes with being an inseparable child of the Most-High God in one lifetime, but I know as I continue to grow in my knowledge of Him, and the greatness of His majesty what I will experience is going to keep me in awe of Him.

Though my wilderness season was brutal, I appreciate every aspect of it. It was necessary for me to go through this process so that I could walk into the promises God had shown me. I discovered that for years I had carried a distorted image of who God was. My time in the wilderness unlocked and released creative areas of my life that I did not know existed and broke false mindsets that were blocking me from realizing the fullness of God. That fullness then illuminated the rest of my life to see the hidden things in my heart.

CHECKPOINT

Think back to a time when you felt like you could not hear God's voice. Even if you never had an experience of hearing His voice know that it's not afar off. What was your spiritual environment at the time? What do you think were some of the traits God was trying to remove or add to your life? Have you had time to sit with God one on one? God is not a fair weather Father but rather love and consistency.

If at any point you cannot hear His voice it may very well be that He is calling you to His presence or calling you deeper in His presence to know Him. Our Father wants to spend time with us to unravel and reveal those hidden parts of ourselves that we did not even know were there. The Lord cares and is intentional about the quality of our spiritual life, so when we go through the pruning process it is never to hurt us but to make us better.

CHAPTER 6

Heart Moves

Throughout my life, I largely dealt with sins of the spirit and heart. These are sins that can't be seen with the naked eye, like bitterness, unforgiveness, anger, and even jealousy. I was holding on to negative feelings which caused me to sin. It is important to remember that God acts directly on the posture of our hearts and is less concerned with our outside appearance. When the Father reveals a character flaw to us, it is done so that we can change the position of our hearts, let go of the flaw, and replace it with the character of Christ. This can be done simply by praying and asking God to remove anything within us that is not like Him. Ask God to replace your weaknesses with His Spirit and His Nature. As God revealed my character flaws, I released them by allowing His nature to live in me.

One situation that I believe the Lord used to reveal my flaws was with a former coworker. For 7 years while working together, Sarah and I battled continually. She would constantly and intentionally try, and sometimes succeed at, causing division between me and our other coworkers. She fed into the usual workplace "he said, she said" drama and tried to make my working experience miserable. Not only would she give off this angry demeanor when I was around, but she would slam equipment down obnoxiously, all in an attempt to get me riled up. On top of all that, she would make false claims about my character, like I'm lazy, confrontational, an all-around bad employee. She would often report me to management in an attempt to get me fired. There were times when we would get into heated arguments, and I would be so annoyed with her antics, that I would retaliate and feed into her petty childish games like leaving more work for her to complete on her shift. It was clear that Sarah and I were never going to be best friends forever!

All of this was going on while I was growing in the Lord. I would ask him, "Lord search my heart, reveal and remove anything that is not like You. Lord replace it with Your nature." Despite my prayers, the conflict with Sarah continued to escalate. I remember one day we got into a huge argument that led to a meeting with our district manager. I was so angry that I decided right then that I would never forgive her for all the unnecessary drama she had caused me.

The next day, as I was driving to Sunday morning service, I clearly heard the Lord say, "Invite her to lunch." My immediate response was, "No, Lord I can't do that!" It hadn't even been a full day after the meeting with our manager; there was no way I was going to swallow my pride or back down. I had resolved that I had every right to be angry, and I was committed to my position on the matter! As I continued to drive, the anger in my heart slowly started to melt away like hot wax. I began seeing Sarah through God's eyes. I still wasn't happy about what He told me to do, but I decided that I would be obedient. Right before I walked into service, I called the store phone because

I knew she was working that morning. I asked her to lunch and she accepted with no hesitation. This didn't surprise me because I knew if God was telling me to do something her response was going to align with what God said. Two days later, we met at a restaurant and talked about our differences. It actually turned into a pleasant conversation, and by the end of the meal, we had enjoyed each other's company. I did not expect it to go as well as it did, but I was glad.

That day I learned how to grant the same mercy, forgiveness, and grace to others, that the Lord grants me every day. Eventually, Sarah and I became cordial, and I extended her an invitation to my church. Even though I was living it, I was blown away by how the relationship between Sarah and I had progressed. I had never expected us to be even slightly cordial with one another, much less have her attend church with me. Having an enemy become a friend is a feeling that I cannot describe, and it was all because of God.

As we walk with Christ, He will slowly reveal things in our heart that we never knew was there. I never knew that I harbored unforgiveness until I had to forgive an enemy. Romans 12:9-21 lays out a blueprint for us to follow when dealing with our enemies. Verse 18 of this chapter talks about living peaceably with all men, which I was willing and eager to do with a person that didn't cause me strife; but, that's not what the scripture says. It says all people! Friends, enemies, coworkers, family, strangers-all people! I had it all wrong. I was willing to extend grace only to those that I deemed deserved it. That's not Christ. If He can forgive those who put Him to death on the cross, I should be able to forgive someone for simply offending me. Ultimately, I learned that His grace is enough for me to overcome any trait that doesn't align with Him. As He reveals to us the impurities in our hearts, let us be intentional and obedient in making the changes He asks of us.

The Lord not only confronted me with the posture of my heart but with the thoughts that lingered in my mind. Ephesians 4:17-24 says that God is concerned with this because in Him we are to be a new creation. 2 Corinthians 5:17 says, "*Therefore, if anyone is in Christ, he is a new creation; old things have passed away; behold, all things have become new.*" This means that when we decide to follow Christ each part of us becomes new and we operate differently from who we were before God changed us.

Numerous scriptures discuss the transformation of our minds. Ephesians 4:23 says, "*...be continually renewed in the spirit of your mind...*" Similarly, Romans 12:2 says, "*Don't be conformed to this world but be transformed by the renewal of your mind.*" Now, I had read those scriptures many times in the past, but the weight of them didn't come to me until the Lord showed me the flaws in my own thinking.

I had considered myself to be an upstanding individual, according to the standards of the world. I did not have any of the usual vices that are normally frowned upon. I wasn't a partier; I didn't drink nor smoke. So, when I decided to follow Christ, I just knew I had an advantage over my peers because I was already doing the "right things." I started to fall into the mindset that my actions made me righteous before God, not considering the fact that the only reason I am made righteous before Him is through His grace and because of the sacrifice that He made on the cross for me. My righteousness was not reliant upon my efforts or doing the "right things". It wasn't until I stopped comparing myself to others and actually measured my life against Christ's, that I saw how much I had missed the mark. I needed to renew my mindset and the way that I viewed my walk with God. The mindset of spiritual superiority is extremely detrimental, especially in cases where the person is not cognizant of their fault.

My revelation and wisdom in the Lord had come so fast, that I started looking down on my peers because they weren't having the same awakenings as I did. I allowed my spiritual haughtiness to become so out of control that I even began comparing myself to my spiritual leaders. Though I was doing the right things on the surface, God sees and searches the heart of men. *"I, the Lord, search the heart, I test the mind, even to give each man according to his ways, according to the fruits of his doings"* (Jeremiah 17:10). If negative thoughts or any form of self-exaltation lingers in our hearts and minds, they will eventually overflow and openly manifest themselves. Mine manifested by me isolating myself from people that I judged to be spiritually immature.

God began to convict me of the thoughts I had towards my peers and leaders. What I was doing was dishonorable before God, and I would never be able to go to the next level harboring these kinds of imperfections in my heart. Hebrews 13:17 tells us, to obey our spiritual leaders and submit to their authority because they are keeping watch over our souls and guarding our spiritual welfare. Although I thought I had submitted to their authority, my thoughts and actions of comparing myself hindered true submission. For months I prayed for promotion in the church because I felt like I was ready to be the leader

I always knew I could be, but when God pulled back the curtains of my heart, and I was able to see who I truly was, all I could do was repent and say, "Lord forgive me!"

Many lessons were born out of this. The first being, never pray for promotion. Promotion is a reward from God. God will openly reward us for the good things we do-with proper intention-that no one sees. Secondly, we should never compare ourselves to anyone. We are all different; that was His perfect design. Just because we may not struggle with the same sins as someone else, does not mean that there are not areas in our lives that need rehabilitation. Thirdly, and most importantly, it is not our place to measure others' spiritual growth, label them, or judge their actions. Although truth and correction should be given when necessary, my job is to live my life in such a way that people see me and ask themselves, *what is different about her? How can I have that peace in my life?* My life should be overflowing with the fragrance of God, so much so, that people are drawn in and want to know how I got to where I am. Then I can share that Jesus is the Rock of my Salvation and that He could be theirs too! My mission is to be a light on the hill- a representative on earth for the Kingdom of the Most-High God.

I counted it a blessing that God didn't promote me while my mind was in that grim condition. Who knows what damage I could have done if I had begun to minister with my heart in that position? Now when I see others not excelling in God, instead of judging them, I pray for them. I ask God to give them a desire for holiness-a desire for Him. I pray that they will give all of themselves to Him, withholding nothing. When I gave God free reign to search my heart and began to live with a changed mindset, is also the moment I laid everything down and carried my cross.

CHECKPOINT

The Lord searches the deepest parts of our hearts. We should be sure to know that just because the outward appearance seems to be intact, God weighs the heart of a man. (Proverbs 21:2)

Check out the story of David and his brothers in 1 Samuel 16. Although the stature of a man is good, God admires a servant's heart. During this time my heart was a mixture of God and self, but we know that one always prevails over the other. How is your heart's posture? Is it fully submitted to God? In this time, I simply said, "Lord search the deepest parts of my heart, reveal anything that is not like You, and replace it with Your Nature."

CHAPTER 7

God's Heart

Throughout the Bible, God's heart concerning His people and the love He has for His children is evident. The Bible gives countless occurrences of people veering away from His statues, holiness, and righteousness, but in turn, God meets them with love, mercy, and grace. God, even in His justness and righteousness, gives ample space for repentance and reconciliation and for people's hearts to turn back to Him. We know that God is good, and we see that goodness through the ultimate sacrifice of sending His Son to pardon our sins and tear the veil that separated us from His presence. Because of that sacrifice, we may now commune with the Father freely.

One thing that I love most about God's heart is His habit of calling people by who He created them to be before they even know it or see it in themselves. Meaning God already knows who he created us to be before we come into that revelation for ourselves. So, God calling us by the purpose He created us to walk in before the foundation of the world is seen multiple times in the Bible. My favorite example of this is Gideon; I feel like I can relate to his life in many ways. In Judges 6, we see the story of Gideon beginning with him in the wine press threshing wheat. As he works, an angel of the Lord appeared before him and said, "The Lord is with you, you mighty man of valor." (Judges 6:12). Gideon's response was that of confusion and disbelief as he questioned if the Lord was really with him and His people. As the Lord told Gideon again to go in his might to save Israel, he met those words with more confusion and doubt. Here we see the Lord gave Gideon two titles that he wasn't familiar with- Mighty man of valor and Might. Gideon did not believe he could do what the Lord was asking of him being from the lessor tribe of Israel and being the least of his tribe. You see Gideon, like most of us, was looking at where he was and assumed that's where he'd always be. Gideon was allowing his present circumstances to define his future. Gideon went on his way, toggling between faith and doubt. We see it in Judges 6:36, where Gideon asks for a sign to confirm that God was really with him. Even though he wavered in his faith he went on to free Israel from their enemies. Thank God for His goodness and that He calls us not by our current condition but by who He predestined us to be. In the beginning, I, like Gideon didn't recognize who, why, and what I was being called. I met God's call for me with question and skepticism, but along the way, I decided to trust Him enough to take steps towards this unknown version of myself. Those steps led me to do what I enjoy doing most, proclaiming God's goodness.

David is another example of God granting a title to someone whose current condition did not resemble God's designation for him. I relate to David also. Although I'm no king or warrior, I am after God's heart. David had flaws like lust, but he was a man after God's own heart. David illustrated this through his reverence, obedience, and faithfulness toward God, but the thing that stood out to me the most was his unconditional love for God. In 2 Samuel 7, we see the covenant that God makes with David. Before the covenant took place, the story reads that David was dwelling in his house after the Lord had given him rest from his enemies. At this time David purposed to build a house of cedar for the Ark of God to dwell. In my interpretation, this was David trying to find a way to bless God as much as God had blessed him. Over the years of David's rule as king, the Lord has abundantly shown David favor and goodness by making him victorious over his enemies. When reading this story, I saw a man whose gratitude and love for God sparked his intention to build this house. God heard David's words and told him that he didn't need a house, but because of David's kind gesture, he makes a covenant with David and his lineage.

Although I never thought to build a house for God, my heart desires to continually give unto Him, to seek Him, to bless Him, and to let Him be Lord over my life. To put a smile on God's face, is my heart's desire. This story also shows us that we can never out-give God. The more we purpose to get closer to God and walk in His ways, the more He will bless us in return. I've learned that by simply delighting in His presence, we begin to uncover the blessings and promises we have in Him and the things He gives freely to us.

Psalm 1:1-3 is a great example of what happens when we delight in God's presence. Verse 2 says, "...but his delight is in the law of the Lord, and in his law, he meditates day and night. He shall be like a tree planted by the rivers of water, that brings forth its fruit in its season, whose leaf shall not wither; and whatever he does shall prosper." A prerequisite to prospering is delighting in the law of the Lord and meditating on it day and night. Imagine whatever you set out to do prospering simply because you decided to put God first.

As you delight in Him, things will begin to progress naturally, like seeking Him and finding Him (Jeremiah 29:13). In seeking Him and His kingdom, all things will be added unto you (Matthew 6:33). My journey started with interest, then seeking, then knowing Him, and lastly, all things being added to me. To clarify, all things being added doesn't mean that all the material things you've ever wanted are miraculously handed to you. What God adds is not of monetary value alone, but spiritual and experiential value- wisdom, clarity, and His revelation of your purpose in life.

Another thing that I love about God's heart is that He's a loving and patient Father. The amount of love that He is ready and willing to pour on His people is unfathomable. "For God so loved the world that he gave his only begotten Son, that whoever believes in Him should not perish but have everlasting life" (John 3:16). This shows us the lengths that God is willing to go to so that we can experience His goodness and reign with Him in eternity. Not only in eternity but we get to experience His love and patience on a daily basis.

How about the story of the lost son? This parable in Luke 15, tells of a story of a man and his two sons. In this story, the younger son asked for his portion of the family inheritance and left the comfort and safety of his father's house to venture out on his own. During his journey, he squandered his inheritance and ended up working in a swine field. The son eventually came to his senses and remembered the overflowing abundance he had in his father's house. As he returned home, his father saw him off in the distance, had compassion for him, ran and fell on his neck, and kissed him (Luke 15:20-21). Not only was the son welcomed back with open arms, but he is met with a celebration. This parable shows the immeasurable love God has for His children. I often wonder how many times this same scenario has played out between God and me, with me thinking that there was something better and more exciting outside the protection of God's kingdom, only to come running back into the safety of His arms.

If this isn't proof enough, the Old Testament is filled with stories about God's love for His people even through their inconsistency, and at times, total disregard of Him (Exodus 16:1-13, Ezekiel 16:1-44; Judges 2:1-5 and Judges 3:7). Although His people's commitment was wavering and indifferent, His love for them never changed. We see where God sent prophets to communicate His displeasure to His people and allowed certain incidents like them being overpowered by their enemies to occur, so that they would remember Him, repent and turn their hearts back to Him. Despite all of their disobedience God never gave up on His people. Many of us have experienced the patience and mercy of God. Even in our broken promises and shortcomings, God remains consistent in His nature and His love for us.

I also love how God never forsakes us. Throughout the Bible, He constantly repeats that He will never leave us nor forsake us (Hebrews 13:5, Deuteronomy 4:31, 31:8, Isaiah 41:10). No matter what was happening, the Lord always reminded His people that He was with them. I find it interesting that in the scriptures where God addresses not forsaking His people, He also addresses fear.

Fear is a spirit that plagues many of us. Fear paralyzes us and stops us from completing our purpose in this world. Joshua 1:1-9 provides a good example of fear and the power it can have over us. In the first nine verses, God tells Joshua three times to be strong and courageous and to not be afraid. He tells Joshua twice, that he will not forsake him. I wonder why God had to repeat himself so many times in one conversation. I believe it's because He knows how easily we can succumb to fear. He knows the areas in which we are fearful, so He addresses them continuously and consistently, to prepare our hearts for what's ahead.

Fear has attacked me all my life-fear of failure, fear of people's perceptions of me, fear of love. It has attempted to stop me from walking in God's promises. To overcome, I had to take hold of God's truth. That truth is that He will never leave me nor forsake me, and because He walks with me, I shall not be afraid. The one thing that fear couldn't do was stop me from carrying my cross.

CHECKPOINT

Who has God called you to be? Did you ever meet what God called you with skepticism and doubt? The Bible lets us know that the Lord knew us and predestined us before we were formed in our mother's womb (Jeremiah 1:5). If this is the case, why do we have such a hard time trusting the words of our God that knew us in eternity? I was there before, and I found my answer to this question to be, I didn't grab a hold of the truth of God. This is an area most, including myself, struggle with. To get me through this hurdle I asked the Lord to show me who I am in Him. I simply say Father, show me the person you predestined me to be and guide me toward that path.

Remember God's heart toward us is to bring us to a prosperous end (Jeremiah 29:11). Knowing all of this and the goodness of God's heart let's trust Him and take those steps to walk into that unknown God-ordained version of ourselves!

"THEREFORE, IF ANYONE IS IN CHRIST, HE IS A NEW CREATION; OLD THINGS HAVE PASSED AWAY; BEHOLD, ALL THINGS HAVE BECOME NEW."

2 CORINTHIANS 5:17

CHAPTER 8

Carrying the Cross

Can you remember a time when your parents and grandparents would drag you to Sunday morning services, or your pastor would say, "You better read your Bible"? I believe one of the reasons they pushed us so hard toward God was because they had tasted and seen that the Lord was good and wanted us to have the same wonderful experiences and encounters with God. What I learned though, is that no matter how much someone may want something for you, you must want it for yourself. Our parents, grandparents, and spiritual leaders cannot carry our cross for us.

The term "carrying the cross" relates to laying down your own will, wants, and desires for your life and following God's will. It is putting everything at His feet and following Him so that His will be done in your life on earth as it is in heaven. We must all make our own commitments to God, as we all have specific destinies and purposes to accomplish here on earth. Only He can reveal and direct us along our paths.

For a long time, I sat on the sidelines during my Christian walk, because I didn't want the full responsibility of following Christ. While watching others, I had seen that following Christ was a way of life that consisted of daily early morning prayer, worship, and days of fasting, not just attending church on Sundays. Like many of us, I wanted all the blessings of a Christian life but saw it as a burden. I saw it as a life filled with restrictions and rules that I wasn't ready to adhere to. I wanted the reward, but not the sacrifice. I wasn't ready to carry my cross at a young age. I had so much life to live-or so I thought- and committing to God would interfere with the things I wanted to do and experience.

Society and the media give us false narratives about life. One of those is that you should spend your twenties partying and socializing, or in other words, "living your best life." It also suggests that around this same time, you should have a career and be "established", otherwise you are a failure. These are two extremes that seem to contradict one another, and Christ is missing in both.

I have experienced feeling burdened by both of those ideas. Personally, I never had the desire to party. It didn't make sense to me to leave the comforts of home to go to an overcrowded club and waste money on overpriced drinks. This was not my idea of fun, but because I wanted to fit in, I did it anyway. I recall a time when I went to a club with a friend and had such a terrible night. I knew I didn't want to be there, so subconsciously, I already knew that I was not going to have a good time. Furthermore, the entire time I was there, something inside of me was urging me to leave. I couldn't enjoy myself even if I tried. After a few more attempts at clubbing, I finally came to terms that it was not my scene. I hung up my stilettos and decided to focus on my education.

In the spring of 2018, I graduated from Rutgers University with a degree in Business Administration and the intent to go to law school. However, I felt like everyone had a head start over me. I was 26 years old, and I didn't have a job that I saw a future in. This was not where I thought I would be at that stage in my life. By this age, I should've had it all: marriage, children, and holding down a profitable career. But here I was, just at step one. I had fully bought into society's ideals.

Somewhere between trying to fit in and trying to plan life, I became truly tired of trying to force myself into a life that I didn't want and tired of what the world had to offer me. So, I stopped trying and leaned on what I knew. I knew God, like many people, through the foundation that was laid on my heart by my elders, through Sunday morning services, through every bible lesson, and through every prayer meeting I was forced to attend.

So, I decided to pick up my cross and follow Him. No longer wavering between Him and trying to fit in with the world. I didn't care what new obstacles came with this decision. I just wanted to walk on the unique path He created for me, not one suggested by the world.

As I grew in God, I saw that this Christian walk has nothing to do with restrictions but with truly knowing the Father and knowing the depth of His love for you. Once I realized that, my heart responded in gratitude and love. Naturally, without me forcing it, things that were not of His nature began to fall away. I didn't mind early morning prayer, worship, and days of fasting, because I desired closeness with Him. In Christ I found peace. I was no longer stressed about timelines or the milestones that I thought I had missed. I knew that He would guide me through to my own destiny-the one that He designed exclusively and perfectly for me. I know now that there is no life outside of Christ.

My questions for you are: Are you truly fed up with what the world has to offer? Can you honestly tell the Lord that you will take up your cross, no matter what comes along with it? Are you ready for Christ to guide you along the journey to who He predestined you to be? Can you genuinely tell Him, "Yes, God! I surrender"?

Carrying the cross is living a life filled with peace in knowing that you are on the path laid out specifically for you. It is a life that will allow you to glorify God through the talents and resources to which He has gifted you. Carrying your cross means that you are secure in knowing that God, our Father, the Creator of the Universe, the King of Kings, first loved you and responding to that love.

Communion With Our Lord and the Holy Spirit

Carrying the cross goes deeper after you say yes to God. When we decide that we want God's will for our lives, there is a natural desire to know Him better. This is where communion begins. In any new relationship, our first inclination is to get to know the other person and to spend time with them. I doubt that just having heard about someone or seeing them on a regular basis, translates to you knowing them. Quality time is the only true way to get to know someone. It is the same way with God. Spending time in his presence and his word will allow us to know him more-first, as our loving Father and then as a lifelong Friend.

I believe a common hindrance in our spiritual growth is that because we cannot physically see God, we tend to prioritize more tangible, day-to-day activities over time with

Him. We may also feel that because God is all-knowing, He must know that we love Him; and therefore, getting to know Him is unnecessary. While it is true that He is an all-knowing God, we still need to make the effort to understand who He is. So, how do we do this? How do we begin to personally know our Father?

In my journey, I worshipped, read the Bible, and created a list of daily confessions that I spoke aloud every day. I committed to rise at 4:30 a.m. for an hour of worship. I started off with worship, because like many of us, I didn't yet know how to study the Bible. Yes, there's a difference between reading and studying the Bible, understanding the revelation behind the words. Worship opened my spirit to have more understanding of the Bible. I would choose a few songs, get on my knees, and sing to God. When I sang to Him, I made sure that my heart was connected to the words.

There were days that I felt like the presence of God was near and days that I felt like I couldn't feel Him at all, but I did not stop. For two months, I stuck to this schedule and then the moment I had been yearning for finally happened. I finally heard God speak to me. He began to pour out His wisdom, and I began to have dreams that could only have come from Him. My Spirit was so sensitive to Him, that throughout the day I could feel His presence and hear Him speak.

Worship brings a closeness with God that is almost unbelievable. I wasn't aware of it at the time, but each day I worshipped I was drawing closer and closer to God's heart. That's why I started to experience all those wonderful moments with Him. I was getting closer to Him, and He was revealing His beauty before me. I was also unaware that when you worship it stirs all the gifts and talents that He placed on the inside of you. Maybe that's where the poetry came from. I truly believe that there is no way we can experience true intimacy and closeness with the Father without worship. Worship is a state of surrender of everything you are before God and glorifying who He is. Worship is such an intricate part of our walk with God; even the throne room of heaven is filled with worship without ceasing (Revelation 4:8-11). Worship opens us up to have confidence in God's word.

After worship, I would dive into the word. Every page in the Bible reveals who God is-His character, His nature, and His thoughts concerning His children. Sometimes I would, and still do, spend hours getting lost in the Bible just reading about His power, dominion, and majesty. I noticed that while I love the entire Bible, I like to spend time in the Old Testament. I like reading how God communicated directly with His people-not only giving them instruction and making covenants with them, but the close relationships He had with certain people like Enoch, Abraham, Ezekiel, Daniel, Elijah, and Samuel. These are all people when reading the word, you can see the intimate relationship they had with God. While there are many more instances of God in relationship with His people, these are the stories that I feel most drawn to. It is so important to remember that the Bible is not just a book, but a living, breathing word, and the only way to activate that word is to speak it. When you speak it, you must know the power behind it, and to know the power behind it, is to know the God who first spoke it.

The Bible doesn't just tell cool stories like David and Goliath, it provides the blueprint for our lives and guides us in prayer. Take for example the model prayer found in Matthew 6:9-13. The disciples asked Jesus to teach them how to pray and He did so by using that prayer. This is the prayer that all believers can begin with. As we continue in our walk with Christ, we may begin to feel burdened in certain aspects of our lives. These are the areas in which we should focus our prayers. Those burdens could be praying for the nation, a loved one, or an enemy. Yes, an enemy; Jesus tells us to pray for them too. It could be anything that the Lord brings before you. In order to know what He's putting before us we must be sensitive to His voice and to the Holy Spirit.

To become more aware of the Holy Spirit's presence we should have a distinct experience. This experience is receiving the Holy Spirit through conversion. This means if we confess Jesus Christ as our Lord and Savior with our mouths, and believe it in our hearts, we will receive the Holy Spirit. At this point according to Ephesians 1:13, we are sealed with the Holy Spirit of promise. Being sealed with that promise means that we are guaranteed our heavenly inheritance at the time of redemption. I believe it's imperative not only to receive the Holy Spirit but to also make sure that we invite the Holy Spirit into every aspect of our lives. The Holy Spirit is many things to us. We need the Holy Spirit in many ways, but one important reason is to reveal Jesus. The Holy Spirit helps to reveal Jesus by opening our eyes to who Jesus is as our personal Lord and Savior and responding to that truth. The Spirit also helps us recognize the personal benefits and eternal gains we have through the sacrifice that Jesus made by dying on the cross. The Holy Spirit opens our eyes to all of this. The work of the Holy Spirit can be found in John 16:6-11.

The Spirit's functions are many in our lives. He is our seal for the day of redemption (Ephesians 1:13-14). He bears witness with our spirit that we are the children of God (Romans 8:14-17). He is our Helper and the Spirit of truth that abides with us forever (John 14:15-18). He is a Teacher (John 14:25-26). He testifies of Jesus (John 15:26). He helps when we don't know what to pray, making intercession for us according to the will of God (Romans 8:26-27). It is evident that the Holy Spirit is a vital part of our walk with Christ. We really cannot go through this journey of serving Christ without the Holy Spirit.

I know that prayer can seem intimidating, but the only way to grow in it is to just do it. Even if you start with one minute of prayer, God sees and will honor your efforts. As you spend more time in prayer, your confidence will increase as you allow the Holy Spirit to guide you in praying for the agenda of God. I learned that it's always beneficial to start prayer with thanksgiving. This simply means that before asking for anything, take the time to recognize and thank God for who He is and what He has done for you no matter how big or small. For instance: "Lord, I thank You for waking me up this morning. I thank you for Your sovereignty. Lord, I thank You for being my Healer, Provider, my Prince of Peace." Once you have thanked Him, ask for Him to lead you in your everyday walk. For example, "Lord, let Your will be done in my life on earth as it is in heaven. Lord let my life reflect who You are." This is just a simple prayer that can be used as a starting point in the early stages of learning how to pray or even beyond. I still use this pattern in my personal prayer life. I believe it's important to note that when praying make it personal with God; speak to Him about whatever is on your heart. Remember He sees your most inner thoughts and know what you need and want before you even verbalize it so don't be afraid to speak to Him from a place of truth. There are no masks and secrets needed in this time with Him.

As we continue to grow in the reading of the word, our prayer language will continue to grow. This means that the more you learn and can recall scripture (God's word), you will better know what scriptures coincide with what you are praying for and can proclaim those scriptures as you pray. For instance, if I were praying for protection over myself or my family, I would start by saying "Lord, thank You for being my Protector." Then I would look for the Bible scriptures that coincide with God's protection over His people. When looking for specific scriptures google is a great tool to use. When flipping through the Bible pay close attention to the headings of the chapters. The heading for Psalms chapter 91 says: Safety of Abiding in the Presence of God (NKJV). After I found that I would read the whole chapter aloud and end with "In Jesus name, Amen!" Likewise, if I am praying specifically for peace, I will use one of the methods I mentioned above. For this example, to search scriptures about peace I used google. First, I typed Bible scriptures for peace. Afterwards I picked a scripture that I felt related to me at that moment. So, in Jeremiah 29:11, it reads "For I know the thoughts that I think toward you, says the Lord, thoughts of peace and not of evil, to give you a future and a hope". (NKJV) Instead of repeating word for word like I did the prayer of protection, I made it my own when talking to God. Starting off I would say 'Lord, thank You for being my Prince of Peace.' Then I would add 'Lord, I thank You that Your thoughts concerning me are of good and not evil, Lord I thank You that You desire to give me a future of hope and a prosperous end. Now Lord I will rest in Your peaceful thoughts concerning me.'

That is just an example of using scripture and making it your own when praying. Prayer can seem intimidating. As we continue to read the word it becomes easier over time. Without realizing it, we begin to store the living word in us and as we pray, we recall and proclaim all that we read over time. This is what happened to me as my prayer life increased in complexity and fervor. The reading of the word not only increased my prayer life, it brought a revelation about who I always was - a Kingdom woman.

CHECKPOINT

Carrying our own cross can seem intimidating but trust me it's not what it seems. I think that a lot of times we walk into this journey with Christ with major misconceptions. I believe the most popular one is that we won't be able to live a fun and thriving life as people who follow Christ. I'm here to say that is false. God cares about your joy and happiness, in fact, He is full of joy, so why wouldn't He want us to have that? Think about what if anything has stopped you from picking up your cross and fully following Christ. What about forming that intimate relationship with Christ, what things if any have hindered you in that area? One thing that I've learned on this journey is that once you wholeheartedly start to follow Christ, true life, freedom, joy, and prosperity begin. We truly have it all in Him!

If you struggle in this area, say "Father, help me to fully surrender my life to You. Let Your presence overflow my life and draw me closer to You."

"DON'T BE CONFORMED TO THIS WORLD BUT BE TRANSFORMED BY THE RENEWAL OF YOUR MIND."
ROMANS 12:2

CHAPTER 9

Kingdom Woman

Spending time with my heavenly Father, learning and relearning His nature has helped me realize who I am and always was. As I grew in the understanding of God's love for me and His purpose for my life it helped me to walk into what I truly am- a Kingdom Woman.

So, what is a Kingdom Woman? Kingdom Women is who we were all meant to be. Women who hear the voice of God. Women that are in tune with the Holy Spirit and uses the guidance of the Spirit to accomplish her God-given purpose- the will of God for her here on earth. She delights in God alone and embraces her uniqueness to glorify God through the gifts and talents He has granted her. A Kingdom Woman has no identity issues and sees herself the way her heavenly Father created her to be. She is a woman that is ready to soar on wings like eagles and let her faith in God order her every footstep. We were all created to be Kingdom Women!

Walking Into Purpose

For a long time, I struggled with this vision of myself as a Kingdom Woman. Although I had grown so much in God and always delighted in Him, I had identity issues. I was not fully aware that effectively living out my purpose was connected to my identity and to the way I saw myself in Christ. Although I felt like I knew who I was, I wasn't fully aware of my worth. Most times, I could not see the beauty of my worth. I could see worth in other women but not my own value.

It's possible that my distorted self-image was a result of my parents' divorce or the hot/cold relationship I had with my dad. But I can certainly trace it back to my youth where my self-image was trampled on by those who should have been caring for me and building me up. As far back as fourth grade, I can vividly remember two incidents where I felt like administrators were attacking me and treating me like an outcast. The first I recall was being purposely locked out of the school building and being separated from the rest of the kids. In fourth grade, I was attending a catholic school. At this school, we had an after-school program where we could play outside for a certain time and then come in and do homework. I don't fully remember if I was being punished but I remember being in the building while the entire group was outside. So, I asked the teacher if I could go outside too, he said sure and then told the whole group to come inside resulting in me being the only kid outside. Now being alone outside I told him I wanted to come inside and then he made everyone go outside. This happened once more before I gave up and just stayed inside by myself. The second incident was particularly disheartening. A teacher's aide looked me in the face and said flatly, "I don't like you". In the same school and grade, my classmates and I had just returned from a day trip at a camp when the aide's granddaughter accused me of breaking a glass mirror in her book bag. I explained to the girl and aide that it could have been anyone since there were 50 backpacks in one pile. Apparently, the aide didn't want to hear it, said her piece, and stared at me while spreading her disgust to her coworker. I had no idea why I was being treated this way and never told anyone about these occurrences. Even though they troubled me, I just sort of rolled with the punches. While my peers were receiving applause, affirmation, and recognition, I received messages of ostracization, dislike, and unworthiness.

Over time, this narrative embedded itself into my subconscious like a worm in an apple, and I perceived myself as unlikeable and unworthy, even when I wasn't being openly judged or treated unkindly. Those crucial years where I should have been building a foundation of self-love and forming a positive image of myself were disrupted before they even began. I believe it was all a part of Satan's ploy to take me out of the game before it started. He shattered any chance of me having a solid emotional foundation by cutting me off from anyone that could encourage or advocate for me. I had no one saying, "You can do it," or "You're enough," or "You're beautiful"! Though these affirmations were used sporadically by my parents, they were never enough to overcome the damage that was being done regularly. This narrative of not being good enough followed me into my twenties until God stepped in and showed me that my beauty, worth, identity, and self-image is found in Him alone. Although the enemy tried to crush my life, God, in His omniscience, had the perfect plan to restore the broken pieces of my image. While God has restored me, learning self-love is still a process that I walk out daily.

I am beginning to see the beauty, worth, and authenticity

in myself. Like so many women, I still fight a mindset that wants to convince me that I am not created in God's image and likeness. I'm still learning that my uniqueness is beautiful, and each one of us is a representative of the various aspects of God's beauty. I can now accept and love the person I was created to be-a Kingdom Woman. I believe that when we reach the point where we see our identity through His eyes, we can flourish in our purpose and individuality in the Kingdom of God.

I think it is necessary to discuss the importance of individuality here. We live in an age where people mask their true selves to look or act like their favorite artist, TV personality, or social media idol. For years, I wished that I could be someone else because I was never comfortable in my own individuality. I would try to imitate women that I thought had everything I wanted. I don't mean just aspiring to have the same success or appearance as these women, but I wanted to be born a different person, to trade lives with these people. I didn't know that I was basically telling God that what He had created, the part of Him that I reflected, wasn't good enough. I did not know at the time that my uniqueness was connected to my purpose, and that it carried a certain capacity, a certain anointing for the things I was called to do.

My uniqueness is a God-given grace that allows me to complete the mission He purposes for my life and glorify Him in a specific way. I didn't understand that I am a specific, unrepeated reflection of Him that no one else can replicate. That is who you are also- a unique, genuine, and perfectly made image of God! The Lord had to totally transform and renew my mind for me to come to this revelation and secure this confidence in who I am. As God began to transform me I could feel the change occurring. I began to see myself in the way he created me to be. This confidence came simply by spending time in His presence. It was as if I began to see through the lens of God.

When walking in this kind of confidence, God's confidence, you feel like nothing can touch you. You have the mindset that you can do all things through Christ. This was a thrilling time for me, because I had never seen myself in this light before. I was finally embracing every part of myself- my nose, my eyes, my wide, size 11 feet. Not only was I accepting my physical features but every aspect of my personality. It was an amazing and exciting feeling. However, walking in this level of confidence can also be a slippery slope. You feel so powerful, that it is easy for pride to seep in; so, when you come to this place of full self-acceptance through Christ, you must strive to maintain a humble heart.

Recognizing that I was a Kingdom Woman and stepping into my purpose was a lengthy process. This was partly due to my own stubbornness and mistakes, but mainly, it was because God needed me to go through this process to get to my purpose. My struggles, lessons, and pain were all leading me on a path to who I am and revealing my destiny piece by piece. God had to fortify me for the future that was waiting for me.

I now see that those years of being an outcast and feeling abandoned were an opportunity for me to draw close to God's heart and allow Him to be the lover of my soul. I now know that those times of famine and going without were preparing me to not only receive the abundance of wealth that God was setting up to pour out on me but teaching me to not put value in money or material things. Now when I receive wealth, I know it's not for my own consumption, but to help those that can't help themselves. I used to be angry and say to God, "Why can't I have a normal life like other people?" I now understand that I am not normal or like everyone else. I have a specific call on my life that required my process to play out in the way that it did, so I can now grab the hands of those that are going through similar situations and inspire and support them to keep going.

I often laugh looking back at my journey and the way God tore down barriers in my life. I was once this shy, timid person who didn't like being around people. Even as a child, I often remember saying that I didn't like kids. I also always said that I would never be a public speaker. The idea of being in front of crowds of people made me nervous. But God is humorous because everything I hated or never wanted for myself is now what I desire to do.

Somewhere during my transformation, I became more social. I wanted to meet and mingle with new people, and now I love kids of all ages. I enjoy being a youth leader at my church and pouring wisdom and knowledge into "my kids". I also plan to establish developmental programs that will assist them in their spiritual growth. I desire now to be bold and courageous for Christ and to go out and proclaim God and all of His goodness to the world. I honestly feel that my love for people was already a part of me, but Satan distorted my view of people at an early age to prevent me from pursuing what God had destined for me-impacting people and kids through the boldness, wisdom, and words He gave me.

Maybe your journey wasn't like mine, but if you reflect on your life lessons, talents, and areas of your life where fear may be lurking, I believe you will find those things that reveal your purpose. Simply say, "Lord reveal my purpose; order my footsteps according to Your will". Despite differing journeys, we have a common goal to glorify God and to let our lives bear fruit in a way that would point others to Christ.

Understanding Purpose

Purpose is simply the reason for which we were born. Once God has shown us our purpose it is then our duty to walk in faith to fulfill it. That means not only having faith that God will guide us through this walk but also understanding our position in Christ. Ephesians 1:20 lets us know that we are seated in heavenly places with Christ, and because of this, everything is already under our feet. This means that we are working from a place of victory in Him and knowing that God has equipped us with everything we need to successfully live out our purposes. As we ask ourselves what we are called to do, remember that the best way to receive this answer is to draw nearer to God's heart. Our vision of ourselves will become clearer as we do this, and then we can guide others that need and want to encounter God.

We all know someone that needs God in their lives. Whether it be for healing, protection, or salvation in general. As Kingdom Women, we are purposed to be intercessors. It is our duty to pray the will of God for people who can't do it for themselves. We intercede on behalf of our friends, family, enemies, and our nation.

Christ's purpose on earth was to intercede for His people.

When He walked on the earth, He showed this by healing the sick, casting out demons, and living a way that people believed He was the Son of God. He made the ultimate sacrifice of dying on the cross, interceding for our sins, so that we can be reconciled back to God. We have the same responsibility as kingdom followers to be verbal intercessors for others as Christ's did for all. This is why knowing our identity in Him is so important. We need to know who we are in Christ and the authority we have that comes with being connected to Him. While this is the general theme of purpose, it differs in the way it is unfolded for each of us. As individuals, we will all be met with different obstacles and barriers that may be a hindrance to us walking in our purpose. But I don't believe the test is whether we can overcome and break through those barriers, but the real test is when purpose takes us on the journey to test our Faith in God.

What happens when purpose, the thing that you believe God has called you to do, doesn't align with your current circumstance or timelines? What happens when your purpose is revealed, but it's not unfolding the way you think it should? How would you react when your purpose impacts your finances in a way that doesn't look like the prosperity God promised you? How about when purpose causes you to stand still and wait on God? Can you trust God in knowing that although nothing looks ideal in the moment, that he's working all things out for your good?

I've faced all of these questions at some junction in my life and at one point all at one time. In the midst of my upset I made the mistake of looking for proof of my purpose in a professional title and salary. In hindsight, this made no sense, as title and salary are not indicative of purpose. While I was focused on finances, I was overlooking how my job allowed me to have deep interactions with coworkers, so that I could pray and intercede on their behalf. Because of the lack of prestige and title, I failed to realize that God had placed me in that position to groom me for my purpose. I was actually doing what He had called me to do, advising and mentoring young women; but I was blind to it because it wasn't panning out the way I envisioned it. You see, I had this fantastic dream of being in stadiums and conferences overflowing with people, on grand stages, ministering to women all over the world, not on a job that I felt stuck in. I was consumed with my vision and my timeline, not giving attention to the Holy Spirit leading me. At one point for me, it became finances versus purpose, and I started seeking new job opportunities. In my search though, almost every door that I tried was closed.

While searching and trying to force my way into job opportunities I hit a huge roadblock. Although it wasn't funny then, I can look back now and laugh at the situation. At one point I was so fed up with the pay at my current job that I purposed in my mind I was going to leave and start a new job. I prayed to God about this job movement. Although I didn't hear Him say "no" I felt a strong push back in my spirit. Just to make a quick notation, God will answer you in some way even if you don't hear His audible voice. In this case, I discerned push back from the Holy Spirit but I disregarded to proceed with my plans. So, in the process of applying to this job suddenly, my knee began to swell. It swelled to the point I could barely walk. You may ask what is the significance here? Well for this job you had to stand on your feet for 12-

hour shifts and walk back and forth throughout the facility. I stopped in the middle of the application process because I knew I couldn't work at a job that requires prolonged amounts of standing with a swollen knee. So, I said to myself when the swelling and pain go away, I will continue with the application process. Well, three days later my leg returned to normal and there I was resuming the process and again my knee started to swell. Frustrated with this occurrence I set an appointment with a specialist. I was determined to get to the bottom of this mysterious swelling. When I went to his office the doctor told me "I see the swelling but theirs nothing wrong with your knee."

I said to him, "clearly there's something wrong" and he said, "no I don't see any problems". Perplexed and annoyed I left the doctor's office. Later that day as I was thinking and frustrated with life, I called it quits on trying to move to that job. Ever since that day my knee has been perfectly fine and hasn't swelled one day since then. Now I'm not insinuating that God is a God that will purposely hurt you, but He does make sure His will and instruction are complete. Consider the story of Jonah and the fish (Jonah 1&2). Here we see how God sent a great fish to swallow Jonah when he ran from God's instruction.

God wanted to teach me a lesson in not finding validation in a job title, but in Him alone. Although my job gave me nothing that I wanted in a professional sense, God used it to shape, mold, and transform my character into what He needed it to be for me to fulfill my purpose. In that position, I learned how to deal with people, to be more forgiving, loving, and increased my faith and peace. My time at that job wasn't done yet and if I had left prematurely it could have hindered my process of maturing in God. While I'm not saying you should stay in a position that is unrewarding or detrimental to you, I am saying to be prayerful as to where God wants you to be and in what season or time frame in your life. God's work in me while I was in that place was unbelievable and a testament to how He can use any platform to promote us. There was, however, one area I continued to battle with is patience.

Because of the constant turmoil in my life, I was always anxiously awaiting the end goal. Trust me if I could fit four years of college into one, I would have found a way to do it. I wasn't a fan of the process or the time it took for things to manifest. Once one goal was accomplished my eyes were set on the next victorious milestone. I had no time to waste. My mindset at the time was to run as fast as I can. While determination is an honorable trait, it is not good to forego rest and deny yourself a moment to bask in what you just achieved. I had to learn the importance and necessity of pausing for a beat, smelling the roses, and enjoying the process. This was not my norm; so automatically impatience crossed over into my relationship with God. Patience and being still in knowing that God is God was a struggle for me. However, when we look at Genesis, chapters 1 and 2, where God is creating the Earth, we see that at the end of each day, even God took the time to sit back and appreciate that "it was good". I wouldn't allow myself that moment, because I thought I needed to run a race to a future that was and is already waiting for me. Letting go of all control and submitting to God to work His perfect plan is now a reality that I've grown to love.

Since we're talking about patience, understanding purpose

also means being aware of God's perfect timing. Everything is purposed for a specific time in our lives. So, if you don't see your purpose manifesting at a certain time, it could simply be that God is still preparing you to emerge in that perfect moment. When you experience what seems to be a roadblock don't grow faint at heart, continue to believe that He is a good Father who desires to bring us to a prosperous end. Let patience have its perfect work. I learned and continue to remember that when walking out our purpose it is so important to be led by the Holy Spirit, allow God to order our footsteps, and most importantly, have patience. That's good advice right! Well, I wish I can rewind the hands of time and minister to my younger self. If that were possible, I would tell her to relax, trust God, and stay in your armor of protection. I would tell her that this walk with Christ is a journey and not a race. I would stress the fact that all the titles and accolades in the world mean nothing if you're not walking in purpose. I would also tell her that even though you will stray a little bit take heart in knowing that God will never let you wander too far before He rails you back in under His hand of protection.

There's a song that when I heard it, forever resonated in my spirit-Mary Mary's "Go Get It". Part of the hook goes, "Go get your blessing! It's your time". I play this song everywhere - at the gym, in times of weariness, or just on a nice drive down the highway. The words give me the strength to keep pressing on and go get the blessings that God already predestined for me. The song somehow speaks to my past and future at the same time, skillfully blending past struggles with a purposed and brighter future.

As I examined my life while not ideal, I see how my journey

was always filled with moments that built my character, faith, endurance, and most importantly, rooted my life in Christ. From the carrying of the cross, revealing of my identity, to the shattering of the false image I unknowingly created of God- He was in control of it all, working all things for my good because I believed in Him. Now I walk with confidence in my identity in Him and am strengthened for what lies ahead. Go getting my blessings means walking on the path that was purposed for me before the foundations of the earth. Every time doubt, fear, or any obstacle rears its head, I remember it's my time. Time to walk as a Kingdom Woman knowing all that I possess in Christ. Time to walk as a woman secured in her purpose. Time to go get the blessings that are waiting for me and I'm sure it's time for you as well.

In my life, I saw that getting the blessing is the easy part. What's hard is constantly choosing to surrender to God's process to transform us into the people ready to receive the blessings He has for us. Lastly, I will reassure her that even through the struggles and circumstances she will encounter in life just keep your eyes on God because He is the great Orchestrator of your life. Everything that He allowed you to go through will only make you stronger and become a part of your testimony. Don't let the frustration from your circumstances derail and out weight what God said or promised you. Be confident in the beauty of your difference because that is where your gifts and anointing unfold. Don't be afraid to follow the specific, untraveled road that God has set for your life.

At times I often questioned the leading of the Holy Spirit because the path He was having me walk down was not parallel to my peers. Often, I thought surely what I'm doing must be wrong because no one I know is walking this path with me. But that's it! This path wasn't carved out for anyone but me just like yours is specifically carved out for you. All this to say know and trust the voice of God in your life. I believe if I could have given my younger self these tips while I was going through my journey, I would have been more at peace going through trials. While it would be ideal to turn back the hands of time, feed off this information, and do it all over again I can't. All I can do is take the lessons, wisdom, and knowledge learned and apply it to the rest of my journey on this walk with Christ. I can tell you that this walk with Christ is not easy, but we have hope and victory because Christ walks with us. If we set in our minds to walk into every obstacle keeping our eyes on God, trusting him, believing that he's guiding your footsteps, speaking faith and life into our situations, and spending time in his presence I know that we will come out victorious on the other side.

There are so many ways that God is prevalent in our lives; His love and the promises of abundance He has set before His people abounds. It would take a lifetime and beyond to experience all His wonders. His character will never change because He is the same yesterday, today, and forever. As we continue to draw close to His heart, let us never forget who He is to us- the love, mercy, and grace He bestows upon us. We do not for our glory, but for His. To let the world know that He is still almighty, He is still sovereign, and He is still seated on the throne.

CHECKPOINT

Do you see the beauty in your uniqueness? Do you know that your purpose is connected to your authentic self? You are a specific, unrepeated reflection of Him that no one else can replicate. God has created us all to represent a specific piece of His beauty and it looks different for all of us. That's why imitating someone else will never bring the fullness you long for, so I've learned. You can never copy someone's identity and that's okay because God gave you your own. Discovering and walking in that identity is something so beautiful. To see who you truly are in God's Kingdom is a vision that compares to none. Our identity in Christ is connected to the authority we have in Him and walking in that authority is awesome! If you are ready to walk down that untraveled specific road that was carved out for you and step into the future that is waiting for you and already yours take that step today. We are all Kingdom Women!!!

Daily Confessions

Here are some daily confessions that helped me walk into the revelation of the person I was always created to be. Remember you can pray anything using "Lord, I thank you." These are just some confessions I made for myself to be rooted in Christ.

- *Lord, I thank You that the I AM is with me.*

- *Lord, I thank You for Your boldness and courageousness.*

- *Lord, I thank You for the freedom to dwell in Your presence.*

- *Lord, I thank You for ordering my footsteps.*

- *Lord, I thank You that I am an ambassador of Your Kingdom.*

- *Lord, I thank You that You have already empowered me to do Your will and I will manifest it on the earth.*

- *Lord, I thank You that You have already empowered me to carry my message and fulfill the mission.*

About the Author

Adasuwa was born and raised in Newark, New Jersey where she attended Newark's Team Academy and later Orange public school systems. During her collegiate studies, she attended Rutgers University in Camden, New Jersey while working a full-time job in order to pay tuition. In May of 2018, Adasuwa earned a Bachelor's degree in Business Administration and plans to put this degree to use soon upon the acceptance of Law School. Ms. Iyamu is community-oriented and one of her primary focuses is to motivate young adults to create a better future for themselves. Currently, Adasuwa is developing a nonprofit organization that will tend to the needs of the inner-city communities.